STAR ★ FILES

Sarah Michelle Gellar

Paul Mason

Raintree

www.raintreepublishers.co.uk

Visit our website to find out more information about **Raintree** books.

To order:

📞 Phone 44 (0) 1865 888113

📄 Send a fax to 44 (0) 1865 314091

💻 Visit the Raintree Bookshop at **www.raintreepublishers.co.uk** to browse our catalogue and order online.

First Produced for Raintree by
White-Thomson Publishing Ltd
Bridgewater Business Centre
210 High Street, Lewes, BN7 2NH

First published in Great Britain by Raintree,
Halley Court, Jordan Hill, Oxford OX2 8EJ,
part of Harcourt Education.
Raintree is a registered trademark of
Harcourt Education Ltd.

© Harcourt Education Ltd 2005
First published in paperback in 2005
The moral right of the proprietor has
been asserted.

Editorial: Nick Hunter and Catherine Clarke
Design: Leishman Design and Michelle Lisseter
Picture Research: Nicola Hodgson
Production: Kevin Blackman
Project Management: Nicola Hodgson

Originated by Dot Gradations Ltd
Printed and bound in China by South China
Printing Company

ISBN 1 844 43831 7 (hardback)
09 08 07 06 05
10 9 8 7 6 5 4 3 2

ISBN 1 844 43838 4 (paperback)
10 09 08 07 06 05
10 9 8 7 6 5 4 3 2 1

927.9143 J

Disclaimer: This book is not authorized or
approved by Sarah Michelle Gellar.

**British Library Cataloguing in
Publication Data**
Mason, Paul.
Sarah Michelle Gellar. – (Star Files)
791.4' 5' 028' 092
A full catalogue record for this book is available
from the British Library.

Acknowledgements
The publishers would like to thank the following
for permission to reproduce photographs: Allstar
Picture Library pp. **13** (l), **14** (l), **15**, **21** (l), **22**
(l), **22** (r), **23**, **25** (l), **26** (r), **27** (l), **30**, **31** (l), **39**
(r), **40** (r); Corbis pp. **6** (r), **9** (r), **10** (l), **20** (l), **20**
(r), **39** (l); Getty Images pp. **7** (r), **12** (r), **19** (r),
28 (l), **29** (r); Retna Pictures pp. **19** (l), **37** (r),
42; Rex Features pp. **5**, **7**, **8**, **9** (l), **10** (r), **11** (l),
12 (l), **13** (r), **14** (r), **16** (l), **16** (r), **17** (l), **17** (r),
18, **21** (r), **24**, **25** (r), **26** (l), **27** (r), **28** (r), **29** (l),
31 (r), **32**, **33** (l), **33** (r), **34** (l), **34** (r), **35**, **36**, **37**
(l), **38**, **40** (l), **41**, **43** (l), **43** (r). Cover
photograph reproduced with permission of
Starmax Inc.

Quote sources: p. **6** interview in the *Chicago Sun
Times*; pp. **8**, **14**, **17**, **18**, **20**, **22**, **28**, **32**, **34**, **35**
Sarah Michelle Gellar, Elizabeth Macdonald;
pp. **10**, **11**, **12**, **31**, **34**, **38** interview in *Star*
magazine, October 2000; p. **19** *Sarah Michelle
Gellar* by Cynthia Laslo; p. **23** *Esquire* magazine,
January 2001; p. **27** www.alwiz.com/bio; pp. **29**,
36, **37** *Teen People* magazine, October 1999;
p. **30** interview in the *Los Angeles Daily News*;
p. **32** Michelle Trachtenberg, *Seventeen*
magazine, August 2001, p. **36** (quotes from
Millar Fuller, President of Habitat for Humanity,
and from Sarah Michelle Gellar) *People*
magazine, September 2001.

The publishers would like to thank Voirrey Carr
and Simone Apel for their assistance in the
preparation of this book.

Every effort has been made to contact copyright
holders of any material reproduced in this book.
Any omissions will be rectified in subsequent
printings if notice is given to the publishers.

The paper used to print this book comes from
sustainable resources.

Contents

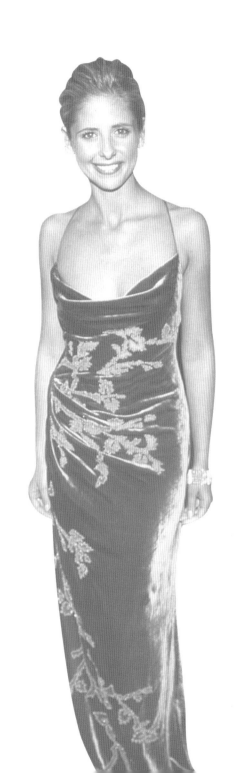

Any words appearing in the text in bold, **like this**, are explained in the Glossary. You can also look out for them in the Star words box at the bottom of each page.

High-kicking heroine

Not many people earn a living by driving stakes through vampire's hearts. That is what Sarah Michelle Gellar – also known as the character Buffy the Vampire Slayer – spent most of her time doing for six years.

ALL ABOUT SARAH

Full name: Sarah Michelle Gellar
Born: 14 April 1977
Place of birth: New York City, N.Y., USA
Height: 5'3" (1.60 metres)
Hair: Dark brown
Eyes: Green
Family: Mother Rosellen Gellar; husband Freddie Prinze Jr.

The Hellmouth

Buffy's high school was located above the 'Hellmouth'. This was a **portal** through which evil creatures could reach Earth. Buffy and her friends spent much of their time trying to keep the Hellmouth closed. They also had to destroy the vampires and **demons** that were drawn to the Hellmouth's energy.

Special talents

Sarah was the perfect actress to play Buffy. One reason is that she has a brown belt in **tae kwon do**. Buffy has to battle vampires and other demons. Sarah's training helped her to act out the fights in a very convincing way. The fights usually end the same way: Buffy wins.

Early starter

Buffy the Vampire Slayer made Sarah Michelle Gellar into a star. She is now famous all over the world.

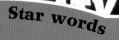

Star words   portal type of doorway. The Hellmouth is a 'doorway' between this world and Hell.

Sarah had been acting for many years before she played Buffy. She first appeared on screen when she was four years old. She acted in an advert. She has worked as an actress ever since.

Other roles

Of course, Buffy and Sarah are not the same person. Buffy is just one of the **roles** that Sarah has played. She has also been in many films. These include *I Know What You Did Last Summer*, *Scream 2* and the *Scooby Doo* films.

Sarah with some of the other stars of *Buffy the Vampire Slayer*.

Find out later

Which fast-food chain sued Sarah when she was four years old?

Which famous US soap opera did Sarah act in?

Which part was Sarah originally chosen to play in *Buffy the Vampire Slayer*?

demons (in *Buffy*) race of beings or spirits that existed on Earth before humans. They are usually evil.

Child star

She's no chicken!

Sarah is a hard worker. She is willing to work long hours until a scene has been shot properly. One advert she did must have pushed her to the limit, though. Sarah had to eat 98 pieces of chicken before the advert makers were happy!

★ ★ ★ ★ ★ ★ ★ ★

Sarah was born on 14 April 1977 in New York City. Her mother is Rosellen Gellar. Rosellen was divorced from Sarah's father in 1984. She brought up Sarah alone. Sarah knew that she wanted to be an actress when she was very young. She got her chance early. Sarah was 'discovered' by a **talent scout** when she was just four.

Sarah grew up in Manhattan, New York.

⭐ Star fact

Sarah first appeared on the US chat show *Late Show with David Letterman* when she was five years old.

Opportunity knocks

The story goes that the talent scout saw Sarah in a restaurant. The scout asked Sarah's mother if Sarah would like to be on television. Sarah stood up and gave her name, address and telephone number. The telephone rang that evening. Sarah was invited to come to an **audition** the next day.

Star words

talent scout someone who looks out for talented performers such as actors, models or athletes

Audition

Sarah went to the audition and impressed the **producers**. She had won her first job. It was an advert for the Burger King restaurant chain. Sarah had taken the first step to becoming a star!

Burger girl

Sarah played a girl enjoying a burger in a Burger King restaurant in 1981. She went on to star in more than 100 different adverts. Even now she is the 'face' of a major cosmetics company.

Sarah made more than 30 adverts for Burger King over the years.

Sarah's good looks make her an ideal choice to be the face of a cosmetics company.

Sarah in court

The Burger King adverts made Sarah's face well known. They caused trouble, too! In the advert Sarah's character said that rival company McDonald's used 'stingy' (small) burgers. McDonald's sued both Sarah and Burger King. Sarah remembers, 'I was telling my friends, "I can't play. I've got to [go and see the lawyers]."'

producer person in charge of making a record, film or television show

★ ★ ★ ★ ★ ★ ★ ★ ★ ★ ★

What's in a name?

When Sarah was six she joined the Screen Actor's Guild. This is an organization for film and television actors. Another actress called Sarah Gellar was already a member. This meant Sarah had to register her full name. This is why she is known as Sarah *Michelle* Gellar.

★ ★ ★ ★ ★ ★ ★ ★ ★ ★ ★

Tough times

Today, Sarah has plenty of money. She has a large home in Los Angeles. She has lots of expensive clothes. It was not always that way, though.

Home alone

Sarah's father Arthur left home in 1984. Sarah and her mother had to survive alone in New York. Rosellen was a **kindergarten** teacher. She and Sarah had little spare money. They struggled to get by. Sarah says, 'We joked that we ate pasta every day for a week, and on Friday night – the big night – we could have macaroni and cheese.'

A close bond

Sarah and her mother went through tough times. This brought them closer together. When Sarah decided to move to Hollywood in 1995, Rosellen moved with her.

" We never owned anything. We struggled for so long. "

Sarah remembers the tough times she had as a child.

Star words

kindergarten nursery school for children of about four to six years old

Sarah's house in Los Angeles is a very different home from her childhood apartment.

Dr Seuss wrote Sarah's favourite children's book. His most famous character is *The Cat in the Hat*.

Still close

Today, Sarah and her mother still live near to each other. They spend time together as often as they can. Sarah also gets on well with her stepfather. Rosellen has been married to him for more than ten years.

Down to earth

Sarah's mother supported her when she was trying to become an actress. She also made sure Sarah kept in touch with her friends. Today Sarah says: 'I've had the same friends forever and I'm very grateful to them, because (me being famous) puts a lot of pressure on them as well.'

Hard worker

Sarah appeared in the films *An Invasion of Privacy* (1983) and *Over the Brooklyn Bridge* (1984). Then she had a break from film work. The film *Funny Farm* was not released until 1988, four years later. Sarah took a break because her mum wanted Sarah to concentrate on her school work.

> When I was growing up, I wish there had been a character like Buffy for me to look up to.

Sarah kept up with her studies while she was becoming well known as an actress.

New school

Sarah remembers this as a happy time. She had some good friends at school. However, she was about to go to **junior high**. Sarah was going to a different junior high from her friends. Now she had earned money from acting, she was going to a private school in New York. She did not know what it would be like.

Sarah made an early appearance in the film *An Invasion of Privacy*.

Spenser: For Hire

In 1986, when Sarah was nine years old, she went back to acting. She appeared in a television show called *Spenser: For Hire*. She played Emily, the daughter of the main character Spenser.

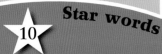
junior high school in the USA for children usually aged twelve to fifteen years old

Spenser was played by a famous actor called Robert Urich. He encouraged Sarah to follow her dream of becoming a full-time actress, once she had finished school.

The Widow Claire

Sarah's next project was also in 1986. She performed in a play called *The Widow Claire* at a well-known New York theatre. The play was about the relationship between a young widow and a college student. Sarah played Molly, one of the widow's two children.

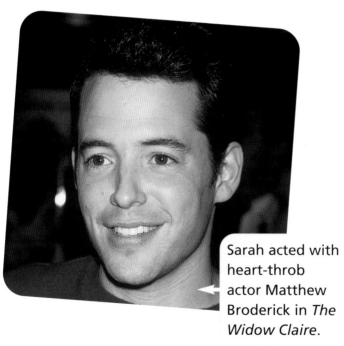

Sarah acted with heart-throb actor Matthew Broderick in *The Widow Claire*.

Exciting time

This was a very exciting time for Sarah. She was also working alongside two young actors who were becoming famous: Matthew Broderick and Eric Stoltz. Sarah later said she was 'the most popular girl in school'.

Bookworm

Sarah has always loved books, especially children's books. She collects **first editions** of books. She has copies of *Alice In Wonderland* and all the books of J. M. Barrie. He wrote the classic story *Peter Pan*. Sarah says that if she were not an actress she would like to write children's stories.

Sarah likes to collect books, particularly first editions.

School years

Sarah started **junior high** at a new school. She went to the Columbia Preparatory School in New York. Most of the students there came from rich families in New York.

Being different

Sarah soon found that she was different from the other students. She was not from a wealthy background. She could afford to go only because of her acting work. Her acting also made her different. It was hard for Sarah to fit in. This was not a happy time.

Tae kwon do

Tae kwon do was great training for Sarah's role in *Buffy* – and her role in the *Scooby Doo* films (above). Tae kwon do is Korean for 'kick punch way'. Sarah has done plenty of kicking and punching in some of her roles!

> " The horrible thing about ... school is that it's about conformity. "

Ice skating was one of Sarah's favourite activities when she was a child.

Star words

conformity fitting in with other people
thriller film filled with excitement and suspense

Chevy Chase was the star of the 1988 film *Funny Farm*, in which Sarah also appeared.

Karate kid

Sarah once finished fourth in the Madison Square Garden Karate Championship. Not many Hollywood stars can say that!

Skating and fighting

Sarah was not only going to school and acting. She also went ice skating. At one time she was one of New York's top figure skaters. Sarah also took up the **martial art tae kwon do** when she was eight. She became good enough to reach the brown belt grade (one of the middle ranks for juniors) by the time she was fourteen. On a busy day, Sarah might start with ice skating, then go to school, then go to **auditions**, and finally do some tae kwon do practice.

Film work

Sarah kept up her film work during this time. In 1988 she was in *Funny Farm* with the famous actor and comedian Chevy Chase. In 1989, she acted with Kathy Bates in a **thriller** called *High Stakes*.

martial art sport or fighting based on a form of self-defence or attack. Tae kwon do, judo and karate are all types of martial art.

13

Teenage trouble

By the time Sarah was thirteen, she was having a tough time at Columbia. 'I never liked to talk about my acting, because if I did I was branded a snob, and if I didn't I was still a snob', she says. Things got really bad when Sarah left town for four months to be in a play. When she got back, she found that her friends at school did not want to spend time with her any more. Sarah says she 'came very close to having a nervous breakdown'.

Future co-star

Sarah went to school in Manhattan with one of her future co-stars, Ryan Phillippe (above). They starred together in *I Know What You Did Last Summer* (1997) and in the 1999 film *Cruel Intentions* (above).

New school

Sarah's mum realized that things had to change. She arranged for Sarah to go to a different school. Sarah moved to the Professional Children's School in Manhattan. This school aimed to help children who had **careers** such as acting, music or sports. Other students included actors Christina Ricci and Macaulay Culkin. Sarah was much happier there.

Like Sarah, Christina Ricci went to the Professional Children's School.

Busy days

Sarah still had a very busy **schedule**. It was becoming impossible for her to do all the things she wanted to.

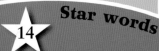

Star words

career job or profession
schedule plan or timetable of events or things to be done

She says 'I would go to the ice rink, then go to school, then go to **auditions**, then go to **tae kwon do**. I was cracking.'

Decisions

Rosellen told Sarah that she could only carry on with two of her four activities. One of them had to be school. Sarah gave up ice skating and tae kwon do. She wanted to focus on acting.

Changing schools

Sarah graduated from the Professional Children's School two years early. She had done very well and had excellent grades. She then went to the LaGuardia High School for the Performing Arts. Here, again, she was studying with other children who worked in show business.

Fame!

The LaGuardia High School for the Performing Arts in Manhattan, where Sarah studied, is a star itself. The school was made famous in the television series, film and musical *Fame!*

The 1980 film *Fame!* was **inspired** by Sarah's school.

inspire give someone the idea or motivation to do something

A Woman Named Jackie

Sarah had decided to concentrate on her acting work. This decision soon had results. In 1991 she was in a US television film called *A Woman Named Jackie*. She played the young Jacqueline Bouvier. Jacqueline Bouvier was the **maiden name** of Jackie Kennedy. She was the wife of US President John F. Kennedy. She was very famous in the USA. Playing Jackie as a young woman was an important **role** for Sarah.

Oscar winner Kathy Bates was once in *All My Children*.

Sarah played Jackie Kennedy (left) as a girl, in a television film.

Swan's Crossing

More acting jobs quickly followed. Sarah won a role in the teen soap opera *Swan's Crossing*. Sarah filmed 65 episodes of the show while she was still at school. She learnt a lot about acting in a long-running show. This was good experience for the six years she spent playing Buffy.

All My Children

All My Children is one of the most successful programmes on US television. It is a soap opera. It follows the lives of people in a fictional town called Pine Valley, Pennsylvania.

Star words   maiden name woman's name before marriage

One of the main characters in *All My Children* is cosmetics **tycoon** Erica Kane. Sarah's next role was playing Erica's daughter, Kendall Hart. Sarah's **debut** as Kendall was on 24 February 1993. Sarah was fifteen years old. Her character was an instant success. Kendall Hart got up to all kinds of tricks. Audiences loved the twists and turns of the plot. Sarah loved the role, too. She says: 'It was amazing playing a psycho-loony.'

Susan Lucci

Sarah appeared in *All My Children* with Susan Lucci (above). Susan played Erica Kane, Sarah's on-screen mother. Susan had been working on the show since its first episode in 1970.

Sarah as the soap opera character Kendall Hart.

tycoon successful and powerful business person
debut first appearance

Sarah's favourite actresses:

Julianne Moore

Stockard Channing

Nicole Kidman

Sandra Bullock.

Daytime Emmy

In 1994 Sarah was **nominated** for a Daytime Emmy for her part on *All My Children*. The Emmy is a major US television award. Sarah had worked on the show for less than a year, so this was a real achievement. Sarah did not win, but the nomination showed how much attention she was getting.

Difficult times

At first, Sarah had got on well with Susan Lucci, who played her mother in *All My Children*. Things changed, though, and the two actresses stopped getting along so well. Sarah found working on *All My Children* harder and harder. She later said that 'It wasn't an easy time in my life. [Susan and I] didn't have a perfect working relationship. We, um, weren't going out to lunch [together].'

Sarah admires Sandra Bullock.

School's out

All the time that Sarah was working on *All My Children*, she was still at school. She finished her final year in 1995. Sarah must have been looking forward to her **prom** night – the traditional party for graduating students in the USA.

★ Star fact

Sarah was once asked which five foods she would need if stranded on a desert island. She said it would be sushi and water five times over!

Party time

There was a problem. Sarah had again been nominated for a Daytime Emmy. The awards ceremony was held on the same night as her prom. What could Sarah do? She says, 'I went to the Emmys and to the after-prom party.' It must have been quite a party. When she got there, Sarah was able to tell her friends that she had won the Emmy. It was also announced that she was leaving *All My Children*. Sarah had proved herself in her home town, New York. Now she was going to Hollywood.

Sarah won her Daytime Emmy award in 1995.

Waterskiing is one of the ways Sarah keeps in shape.

An active life

Sarah works very hard. To keep her energy levels up, she takes **power naps** through the day. For exercise she goes to the gym, or works out at home. She also enjoys yoga, rollerblading and waterskiing.

Moving to L.A.

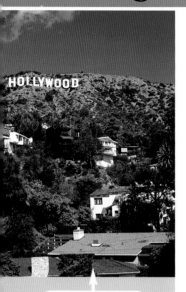

Sarah and Rosellen moved to Los Angeles together when Sarah finished school in 1995. Sarah's mum is not like a manager. She did not push her daughter towards an acting career. In fact, Sarah says that if she wanted to give up acting, her mum would support her.

Sarah and her mum moved to Hollywood in 1995.

Living in L.A.

Sarah has lived in Los Angeles for years now. Rosellen's house is just five minutes away from Sarah's home. They try to spend time together every week. Sarah says, 'It's always been the two of us, so we've learned to depend on each other and help each other. There's nothing I can't discuss with my mother.'

Buffy beckons

Sarah must have needed her mum's support when they first arrived in Los Angeles. It took a while for her career to get going. Then Sarah's luck changed. She was asked to **audition** for a part in a new television series. The series was about a group of high-school kids who battle the forces of evil. It was called *Buffy the Vampire Slayer*.

Thriller chiller

Sarah's part in *Buffy* meant she spent a lot of time fighting vampires, often in graveyards at night. It is a good job that Sarah did not reveal her worst fear at the audition – it is graveyards!

Sarah is scared of graveyards!

Star words

Kristy Swanson played Buffy in the original film version.

Buffy's creator

Joss Whedon is the creator of *Buffy*. He wrote the original film version of *Buffy the Vampire Slayer*. He has also written the scripts for big Hollywood films like *Alien: Resurrection*, *Toy Story* and *Speed*.

Joss Whedon dreamt up *Buffy* and wrote many of the episodes.

The first Buffy

There had already been a film version of *Buffy the Vampire Slayer*. This was released in 1992. Kristy Swanson had played the part of Buffy. Now the creators wanted to turn it into a television series.

Cordelia or Buffy?

Sarah was asked to audition for the part of Cordelia. Her character starts out as a snobby popular girl. She makes fun of Buffy and her friends. Sarah was offered the part, but was afraid of being **typecast** if she played another **role** like the spoilt Kendall Hart. Two weeks later, though, the phone rang again. Would Sarah come back and audition for the role of Buffy?

typecast when an actor is given very similar roles to play, over and over again

Buffy the Vampire Slayer

Buffy with her 'Watcher', school librarian Rupert Giles.

★ ★ ★ ★ ★ ★ ★ ★ ★ ★

Chosen One

Buffy is famous for its snappy **dialogue**, as these lines from the first-ever episode show: Giles: 'Into each generation a Slayer is born. One girl, in all the world, a Chosen One. One born with the…' Buffy: '… the strength and skill to hunt the vampires, to stop the spread of evil, blah blah. I've heard it, okay?'

★ ★ ★ ★ ★ ★ ★ ★

Joss Whedon is the creator of *Buffy the Vampire Slayer*. He remembers Sarah's final **audition** for the part. 'She gave us a reading that was letter perfect. And then said, "By the way, it doesn't say this on my **résumé**, but I did take **tae kwon do** for four years and I'm a brown belt. Is that good?" No, I thought, it's perfect.' Sarah was offered the part.

The girl in the alleyway

Joss Whedon says that the original idea for Buffy came from horror films. He thought about a typical character in a horror film – a girl who goes down a dark alleyway and gets killed. Whedon wanted to change that. He imagined having a tough heroine, like Buffy.

Buffy is helped in her fight against evil by other members of the 'Scooby Gang'.

dialogue speech between two or more people
résumé list of jobs and skills

'I just had that image, that scene, in my mind, like the **trailer** for a movie – what if the girl goes into the dark alley? And the monster follows her? And she destroys him?'

Welcome to the Hellmouth

The first episode of Buffy is called 'Welcome to the Hellmouth'. Buffy Summers arrives in the town of Sunnydale. She has been expelled from her old school for burning down the gymnasium. This happened in the fight against vampires, in her job as the Slayer. She then finds out that Sunnydale High is located above the 'Hellmouth', which could destroy the world if it were opened.

The Slayer

Buffy is a vampire slayer. At first she is the only Slayer, because there is meant to be only one in each generation. The school librarian, Rupert Giles, is waiting in Sunnydale to become Buffy's Watcher. He guides her in the fight against evil. Buffy also battles with the vampires and other **demons** drawn to the Hellmouth's evil energy.

Vampire language:
• feeding – drinking blood, a vampire's food
• The Master – the oldest and most powerful of all the vampires
• sire – to 'sire' is to make someone into a vampire
• Slayer – girl with the ability to hunt and kill vampires
• vampire – an undead creature that appears human until it feeds (see above), when it shows its true vampire face.

Angel

Angel became the star of his own **spin-off** series. Angel is a vampire who is hundreds of years old. Because of a gypsy curse, Angel has a soul, which stops him from being evil. Before he leaves the series, Angel becomes Buffy's boyfriend. A vampire going out with a Slayer? Yes, it gets complicated.

Buffy's success

Buffy made Sarah and the other actors who starred in the show famous. Audiences loved the blend of real-life situations with fantasy and horror. Buffy and her friends do not just have to fight against the **supernatural** forces of evil. They have to deal with being in high school, too. Sometimes this seems harder.

Critics corner

Buffy was loved by most television **critics**, as well as by people watching at home. Critics praised the way the actions of the characters had long term, realistic consequences. Buffy, for example, spends so much time slaying vampires that when she finishes school she cannot get a well-paid job.

Buffy's helpers

Buffy is helped in her battle against evil by a group of friends. Willow, played by Alyson Hannigan, uses magic to help Buffy. Other characters include Xander (played by Nicholas Brendon) and Buffy's Watcher, Rupert Giles (played by English actor Anthony Stewart Head). Two of the main vampire characters are Angel (played by David Boreanaz) and Spike (James Marsters). Both Angel and Spike are 'good' and 'bad' vampires during the series.

David Boreanaz plays the vampire Angel.

Star words critics people paid to review entertainment such as films or television programmes

Ghost of the Robot

James Marsters plays the vampire Spike. After the last-ever series of *Buffy*, Spike joins Angel in Los Angeles. Marsters is multi-talented. He is also part of a band called Ghost of the Robot.

Buffy threatening to drive a stake into the vampire Drusilla's heart.

Alyson Hannigan

Sarah and Alyson Hannigan (below) are friends in real life, as well as on *Buffy*. Like Sarah, Alyson started acting as a child. She got her first job when she was just four years old.

spin-off television series featuring characters that were originally in a different television series

James van der Beek starred in *Dawson's Creek* and appeared in *Scream 2*.

The 'Dawson' connection

I Know What You Did Last Summer and *Scream 2* were both written by Kevin Williamson. Williamson first became famous as the scriptwriter on *Dawson's Creek*.

This scene shows Sarah in *I Know What You Did Last Summer*.

Long days

Working on a show like *Buffy* might seem glamorous, but it is also very hard work. Sarah often had to work long days while filming. Lots of the scenes were shot at night – since that is when vampires come out. Sometimes shooting would not finish until midnight or later.

Scream queen

The first series of *Buffy* was made in 1996–97. Many actors would have taken a break when the filming finished. Not Sarah: she had two film parts, both in horror films. The first was called *I Know What You Did Last Summer*. Sarah played one of a group of four friends. While out celebrating their graduation, they run down and kill a walker. They do not tell anyone about the crime. They dump his body in the sea instead. The next summer, one of them gets a letter. It says 'I know what you did last summer'.

Star words

box office place where tickets are sold. If a film does well at the box office it means that a lot of people paid to see it.

The friends try to find out who knows their secret. Sarah's character, Helen Shivers, is killed during the film.

Scream 2

Next Sarah acted in a film called *Scream 2*. She only had a small part, which was just as well. The filming began at almost the same time as work on the second series of *Buffy*. Again, Sarah's character did not live to the end. This time she fell off a balcony trying to escape. *Scream 2* was a huge success. It made about US$96 million at the **box office** in its first month.

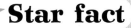
★ Star fact

Sarah loves horror films. She does not mind if her horror film characters get killed. She once said: 'I want it to be really gory. Body parts all over the place. Mangled!'

Sarah met Freddie Prinze Jr while making *I Know What You Did Last Summer*.

Romance on set

One of Sarah's co-stars in *I Know What You Did...* was Freddie Prinze Jr. The two got on well. Later they got on even better. They were married on 1 September 2002.

Sarah had a small part in the popular film *Scream 2*.

Worldwide success

Buffy soon became very popular. At first it was only seen in the USA. By the end of its second series, *Buffy* was the most-watched programme on US television. Soon *Buffy* was shown all over the world. Sarah was the star of the show. This meant she was at the centre of all this success. She did not have much time to enjoy it, though. As she said in an interview: 'Basically, my life is just work, work, work!' Fortunately, Sarah has also called herself 'the type of person who gets bored if I don't work for two days'.

Sarah goes to the same gym as basketball star Shaquille O'Neal.

★ ★ ★ ★ ★ ★ ★ ★ ★ ★

Shaq attack!

Sarah takes keeping fit very seriously. She tries to go to the gym three or four times a week. One of her training partners at the gym is Shaquille O'Neal. He is a star player for the L.A. Lakers basketball team.

★ ★ ★ ★ ★ ★ ★ ★ ★ ★

Signing autographs is part of the job for any successful actress like Sarah.

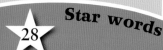

Star words

28

media ways of communicating with lots of people, such as television, radio and newspapers

Keeping fit

Sarah performs a lot of Buffy's kicks, spins and punches herself. A stuntwoman performs Buffy's more dangerous stunts. She also runs around a lot as part of the action. With such a demanding job, it is important for Sarah to keep fit. She visits the gym regularly, and sometimes works out at home.

> There's no question I live a very, very strange life.

The price of fame

There are disadvantages to being famous. It can be hard to get away from the **media** and relax. After filming *Scooby Doo* in Australia, Sarah remembered that 'sometimes it was hard to get a cup of coffee without worrying about being followed or tracked down'.

It is hard for Sarah to be a private person. Here, she is running away from a photographer.

Sarah's singing featured on the album from the musical episode of *Buffy*.

Singing star

Sarah finds it relaxing to sing a bit of **karaoke**. One episode of *Buffy*, called 'Once More, With Feeling' was followed by an album of the soundtrack. Sarah sings on several of the songs.

Hits and misses

★ ★ ★ ★ ★ ★ ★ ★ ★ ★ ★

Reviews

Reviewers were not very kind to *Simply Irresistible*, in which Sarah played a chef. One review included food-based comments such as 'falls like a soggy soufflé' and 'no spice, no zest, no originality'.

★ ★ ★ ★ ★ ★ ★ ★ ★

Sarah plays a chef in the film *Simply Irresistible*.

Every big star like Sarah has been in lots of successful shows and films. Most have also been in a few **turkeys**, playing parts they would rather forget. While Sarah was filming *Buffy*, she also acted in a film that showed that even she cannot make everything a hit.

Simply Irresistible

In 1999 Sarah appeared in *Simply Irresistible*. She played Amanda Shelton, a chef in a restaurant. The film is a romantic comedy. Sarah's character tries to find love with a businessman played by Sean Patrick Flanery. The film **bombed**. Sarah later said that 'it didn't turn out to be the movie we set out to make … hopefully it didn't do me too much damage'.

Star words   turkey film that few people went to see
bombed very unsuccessful

30

Cruel Intentions was a hit film for Sarah.

Love twist

Two of Sarah's co-stars in *Cruel Intentions* were real-life couple Ryan Phillippe and Reese Witherspoon (below). They had first met in 1997. They fell in love and were married in 1999. In October 2003 their four-year-old daughter Ava got a baby brother, Deacon.

Cruel Intentions

Things got better later in 1999 when Sarah made *Cruel Intentions*. The film was about a stepbrother and sister who like to make trouble. Sarah starred with former classmate Ryan Phillippe. Reese Witherspoon and Selma Blair took the other main roles. *Cruel Intentions* was a great success.

Playing a baddie

Sarah's experience as a baddie in *All My Children* must have helped her to play the part of Kathryn Merteuil in *Cruel Intentions*. She won good reviews. People who only knew her as Buffy realized that Sarah had a much wider **acting range**.

acting range ability to play a wide variety of different characters

Away from the studio

In public

At major awards ceremonies or at big public appearances, Sarah often looks very glamorous.

★ ★ ★ ★ ★ ★ ★

As Buffy, Sarah looked good even when she was fighting vampires. Buffy's clothes were chosen by a professional **costume designer**. Her outfits made her look well dressed, but in affordable clothes. In reality, many of them came from designer labels.

Sarah's style

Sarah creates a style that is all her own. She mixes clothes from her favourite designers with **vintage clothes**. Sarah says that she likes 'any clothes that are comfortable and kind of funky'. Her fashion advice is: 'Long leather coats. There's nothing better. You put one on, you always look good.'

★ Star fact

Sarah is famous for giving excellent barbecue parties, with lots of meat on the grill.

Dressing down

When she is not out in public, Sarah's wardrobe is very different. She likes to dress in a way that avoids attention. Sarah wears comfortable clothes when she's at home. She says 'I'm a baseball hat and overalls girl at the weekends.'

Trend setter

Michelle Trachtenberg, who played Buffy's younger sister Dawn, says: 'Sarah knows what the next trend will be. She's always saying, "No, honey, that's not cool anymore." She's the fashion queen.'

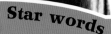
costume designer person who chooses what actors wear on set

Body decoration

Sarah once wore a ring in her belly button. She also has five earring holes in each ear. She has several tattoos. There is a Chinese symbol for 'patience' on her ankle. She also has a symbol for '**integrity**' on her lower back and a Celtic shape on her left hip.

Portishead is one of Sarah's favourite bands.

Desert island discs

If she were stranded on a desert island, Sarah would take these CDs:

Portishead's Dummy

Cree Summers' Chess

Anything by Stevie Wonder

Talking books of all the Harry Potter stories.

Away from the spotlight Sarah is still stylish but much more relaxed.

---

vintage clothes good-quality secondhand clothes
integrity honesty

True romance

Sarah has said that it was hard for a successful actress like her to have a boyfriend. She once said that 'It's very, very difficult for me whenever I get into a relationship, because of the insane hours I work … I can go for three weeks and not speak to anyone, which can be really difficult.'

Freddie's father, Freddie Prinze Sr.

Sarah with her husband Freddie Prinze Jr.

★ ★ ★ ★ ★ ★ ★ ★ ★ ★

Freddie Prinze Sr

Sarah's husband Freddie is the son of a famous 1970s actor and comedian, also named Freddie Prinze. His dad died when Freddie was still a baby. Sarah too spent part of her childhood without a father. Her dad left home when she was a small girl.

★ ★ ★ ★ ★ ★ ★ ★ ★ ★

Star words celebrity famous person

Celebrity partners

A lot of famous people go out with other **celebrities**. Sometimes this might be for **publicity** purposes. It means that both people might get their photos in magazines. Sarah says that there are other reasons why celebrities go out with each other: 'A bad day in show business is a lot different from a bad day anywhere else. It takes someone who's been through it to understand.'

Marriage

In 1997 Sarah met the actor Freddie Prinze Jr. They worked together on the film *I Know What You Did Last Summer*. A romance blossomed between them. They were married in Mexico in September 2002.

⭐ **Star fact**

Sarah once bought Freddie a detailed map of Los Angeles. She was fed up of Freddy being late to dates because he could not follow directions!

Working together

Both Sarah and Freddie are popular actors. Each works away from home for long periods of time. It can be difficult for them to spend time together. Perhaps they will try to act in the same films together, as they did in the *Scooby Doo* films.

Sarah with Freddie on the set of her 2001 film *Harvard Man*.

Inspiration

Sarah knew before she got married that it was possible to be married to a fellow actor. She had seen it with her *Cruel Intentions* co-stars Reese Witherspoon and Ryan Phillippe. Sarah says, 'They're an **inspiration** to young love.'

Hollywood influence

The president of Habitat of Humanity says: 'Sarah's involvement really telegraphs a powerful message... that this is a good thing to do... She's willing to get her hands dirty, and that's impressive.'

Like Sarah, the famous actress Susan Sarandon works for the Habitat of Humanity charity.

Charity work

Sarah is involved with several charities. She tries to help people who are less fortunate than herself. She donates money, like many Hollywood stars. Sarah also helps by joining in on some of the charities' projects.

The Starlight Foundation

One of the charities Sarah helps is the Starlight Foundation. Many **celebrities** support this charity. The Foundation works with seriously ill children, especially those in hospital. Its main aim is to help children and their families by cheering them up and taking their minds off their illness.

Habitat of Humanity

Habitat of Humanity builds or **renovates** simple homes for homeless people. Charity **volunteers** work alongside the people who will live in the homes they are building. Sarah has done her part, working on the building site with other volunteers. Sarah says: 'I'm not going to find a cure for cancer. That's not an ability I have. But I can donate money that will help with research, and I can really do something here.'

> ★ **Star fact** The magazine *Teen People* in October 1999 described Sarah at work for Habitat of Humanity: 'With one shoe untied and damp spots on her pants showing where she has wiped her hands, a disheveled Sarah joins the bucket brigade.'

Star words   renovate rebuild or improve

Sarah also helps raise money for the breast cancer charity Young Survival Coalition.

Sarah the Builder

One of Sarah's first jobs for the charity Habitat of Humanity was in the Dominican Republic. She helped a family to mix and lay cement as the foundation for their new home. Who says Hollywood stars do not like to get their hands dirty?

Harrison Ford is another City Harvest supporter.

City Harvest

Sarah also supports City Harvest. This charity began in New York. The charity collects leftover food from restaurants, schools and businesses. The food is then distributed to homeless people. Without the charity's work these people would go hungry, and the leftover food would be wasted.

Life after Buffy

★ ★ ★ ★ ★ ★ ★ ★ ★ ★

Snappy scripts

Some of the great lines that Buffy said include:
• 'You're a vampire. Oh, I'm sorry. Was that an offensive term? Should I say undead American?'
• 'I can beat up the demons until the cows come home... and then I can beat up the cows.'
• 'That probably would've sounded more convincing if I wasn't wearing my yummy sushi pajamas.'
• 'Hi I'm Buffy... and you're history.'

★ ★ ★ ★ ★ ★ ★ ★ ★ ★

Sarah and her fellow actors filmed the final episode of *Buffy* in 2002. The team from Sunnydale have now killed their last vampire together.

Buffy love

Buffy was one of the few television series that both audiences and **critics** loved. There are websites, magazines and books about the series. So, why was *Buffy* so popular?

Girl power

One reason for the show's success is the female characters. The girls in *Buffy* are strong, brave and funny. Audiences loved to watch the heroines in action. As Sarah once said: 'Women can handle things and be perfectly capable. That's the reason why I think the Spice Girls or *Buffy*, or *Ally McBeal* [did] so well. Women can really look up to these people.'

Sarah thinks the Spice Girls **inspired** girls just as Buffy did.

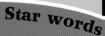
Star words   gothic type of fiction that includes elements of horror

Imagine studying *Buffy* at university! Well, in Australia you can.

Buffy studies

Do you want to study Buffy? Try the University of Adelaide in Australia. There is a course called '**gothic** literature and **pop culture**'. It includes a unit on *Buffy*. It is very popular. In the first term, 225 out of 304 students took the *Buffy* option.

Real life

Many critics like the way that *Buffy* reflects real-life situations. (Not the Hellmouth, vampires and **demons**, of course.) Buffy and her friends have real problems, with friendships, boyfriends and girlfriends, school and family life.

Ordinary kids

The characters also share the same interests as ordinary teenagers. In one episode, Willow and Buffy exchange some classic lines after their enemies have run away from them:
Willow: 'Oh my God, Buffy!'
Buffy: 'I know, they're gone. I guess we should chase them.'
Willow: 'No, your hair! It's adorable!'

Audiences love the fact that Buffy is a beautiful girl who can also fight.

pop culture to do with popular films, books, magazines and other entertainment

Buffy's done

By the autumn of 2002, Sarah was one of the most popular actresses around. The final series of *Buffy* was about to be screened. In June, Sarah's latest film, *Scooby Doo* came out. It had one of the most successful **opening weekends** in history.

The original *Buffy* gang.

Scooby Gang

There is a link between *Buffy* and *Scooby Doo*. Sarah's gang of friends and helpers in *Buffy* called themselves 'The Scooby Gang' after the kids in the *Scooby Doo* cartoons.

The main characters of the film *Scooby Doo*.

Star words opening weekend first weekend that the public can go to see a film

The Scooby Doo films

Scooby Doo also starred Sarah's husband, Freddie Prinze Jr. The two played Fred and Daphne, members of Mystery Inc. Mystery Inc. is a group of four friends, plus Scooby Doo the dog. They find out the truth behind strange events. The film was based on a successful cartoon from the 1970s. **Critics** did not like *Scooby Doo*, but audiences loved it. The film was so successful that a sequel was made. *Scooby Doo 2: Monsters Unleashed* starred Sarah and Freddie again. The film came out in 2004.

Harvard Man

Another of Sarah's films was very different from *Scooby Doo. Harvard Man* (2001) was a comedy for adults. The film's main character, Alan, is a university student. He gets involved with a cheerleader called Cindy (played by Sarah). Alan does not know that Cindy's dad is a member of the **Mob**. Things start to go wrong for Alan. He ends up trying to outsmart Cindy, her dad and the FBI. Playing Cindy was another new type of part for Sarah. It showed again that she is an actress who can play lots of different **roles**.

Scooby Doo: the plot

In the first film, Mystery Inc. go to Spooky Island. They want to solve the mystery of what seem to be **supernatural** events. The island's owner wants to know why holidaymakers are being turned into **zombies**. Not everything is what it seems ... but by the end Mystery Inc. find out who the real villain is.

Sarah in a scene from the film *Harvard Man*.

Versatile voices

Sarah has given voices to several cartoon characters. Her voice was in *Small Soldiers* and the television show *Hercules*. In 2004 she did a **voice-over** for *Happily N'Ever After*. This is a cartoon version of the Cinderella story. The film also stars the voice of Freddie Prinze Jr.

Sarah with her co-host Jack Black at the MTV movie awards.

New horizons

When *Buffy* finished, Sarah might have felt like taking a break. This was almost the first time since *All My Children* in 1995 that Sarah had not been working on a regular television series. Sarah has kept as busy as ever, though.

Future projects

In 2004, Sarah starred in another horror film, *The Grudge*. She is also lined up to make a film called *Romantic Comedy*. She must be hoping that it will be more popular than her last romantic comedy, *Simply Irresistible*. When she was young, Sarah liked to do lots of different things. She was busy with ice skating, **tae kwon do** and acting. Today, she still likes to have a varied life.

Hosting

Sarah has worked as a television host. She has been on the comedy show *Saturday Night Live* several times. After Sarah's first appearance, **ratings** for *Buffy* grew by over a million viewers. Sarah has also hosted major awards ceremonies, including the MTV movie awards.

Star words

voice-over voice given to a cartoon character
ratings numbers of viewers

In 2002, she appeared in two short films for the Awards: *Jack Black: Spiderman* and *Lord of the Piercings*. This last one was a **spoof** of the film *Lord of the Rings*.

Guest appearances

Sarah sometimes appears as a guest on other shows. She has been in the cartoon *King of the Hill* and the comedy series *Sex and the City*. Sarah has also been in some episodes of *Angel*.

Fans approach Sarah for her autograph all the time.

Sarah pretending to be Christina Aguilera on the comedy show *Saturday Night Live*.

★ ★ ★ ★ ★ ★ ★ ★ ★

Fighting dog

Sarah has a dog called Thor. He is a Maltese terrier. He came with Sarah when she was filming *Buffy*. He would watch all the scenes except the fight scenes, when he would bark loudly then leave the set. Sarah now has another dog, too. It is an Akita named Tyson.

★ ★ ★ ★ ★ ★ ★ ★

spoof comedy version

Find out more

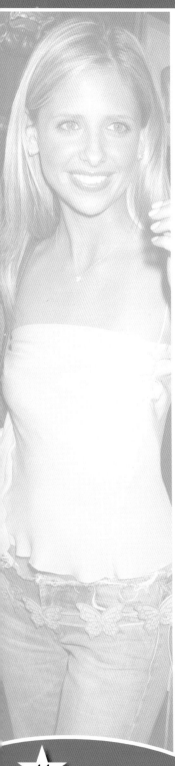

Books

Buffy the Vampire Slayer: The Watcher's Guide
   Christopher Golden and Nancy Holder
   (Pocket Books, 1999)

*Buffy the Vampire Slayer: The Watcher's Guide
   Volume 2*, Nancy Holder with Jeff Mariotte and
   Maryelizabeth Hart (Pocket Books, 2000)

Celebrity Bios: Sarah Michelle Gellar, Cynthia
   Laslo (Children's Press, 2000)

*The Girl's Got Bite: The Original Unauthorized
   Guide to Buffy's World*, Kathleen Tracy
   (Griffen, revised and updated edition, 2003)

Sarah Michelle Gellar, Elizabeth Macdonald
   (Carlton Books, 2002)

Filmography

Southland Tales (due 2006)

The Grudge 2 (due 2006)

2004: A Light Knight's Odyssey (due 2006)

Happily N'Ever After (2005)

The Grudge (2004)

Scooby Doo 2: Monsters Unleashed (2004)

Scooby Doo (2002)

Harvard Man (2001)

Cruel Intentions (1999)

Simply Irresistible (1999)

Small Soldiers (1998)

Scream 2 (1997)

I Know What You Did Last Summer (1997)

High Stakes (1989)

Funny Farm (1988)
Over the Brooklyn Bridge (1984)
An Invasion of Privacy (1983)

Television
Buffy the Vampire Slayer (1996–2002)
All My Children (1993–95)
A Woman Named Jackie (1991)
Swans Crossing (1990–91)
Spenser: For Hire (1986)

Websites
To find out more about *Buffy the Vampire Slayer*, try these sites:

http://www.bbc.co.uk/cult/buffy
http://www.buffy.com

To find out more about Sarah try this site:
http://www.smgfan.com

Disclaimer
All the Internet addresses (URLs) given in this book were valid at the time of going to press. However, due to the dynamic nature of the Internet, some addresses may have changed, or sites may have ceased to exist since publication. While the author and publishers regret any inconvenience this may cause readers, no responsibility for any such changes can be accepted by either the author or the publishers.

acting range ability to play a wide variety of different characters

audition interview for a musician or actor, where they show their skills

bombed very unsuccessful

box office place where tickets are sold. If a film does well at the box office it means that a lot of people paid to see it.

career job or profession

celebrity famous person

conformity fitting in with other people

costume designer person who chooses what actors wear on set

critics people paid to review entertainment such as films or television programmes

debut first appearance

demons (in *Buffy*) race of beings or spirits that existed on Earth before humans. They are usually evil.

dialogue speech between two or more people

first edition first printing of a book

gothic type of fiction that includes elements of horror

inspire give someone the idea or motivation to do something

integrity honesty

junior high school in the USA for children usually aged twelve to fifteen years old

karaoke singing along to famous songs that are played without the words

kindergarten nursery school for children of about four to six years old

maiden name woman's name before marriage

martial art sport or fighting based on a form of self-defence or attack. Tae kwon do, judo and karate are all types of martial art.

media ways of communicating with lots of people, such as television, radio and newspapers

Mob US criminal organization also known as the Mafia

nervous breakdown period of mental illness usually caused by stress or depression when someone is going through a hard time in their life

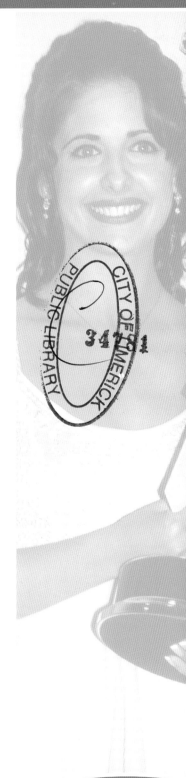

nominated to be put forward as one of the people to win an award

opening weekend first weekend that the public can go to see a film

pop culture to do with popular films, books, magazines and other entertainment

portal type of doorway. The Hellmouth is a 'doorway' between this world and Hell.

power nap short sleep of about 30 minutes to keep energy levels up

producer person in charge of making a record, film or television show

prom party for graduating students in the USA

publicity becoming well known

ratings numbers of viewers

renovate rebuild or improve

résumé list of jobs and skills

role part that an actor plays in a film, play or television show

schedule plan or timetable of events or things to be done

spin-off television series featuring characters that were originally in a different television series

spoof comedy version

supernatural not from the natural world

tae kwon do Korean system of self-defence

talent scout someone who looks out for talented performers such as actors, models or athletes

thriller film filled with excitement and suspense

trailer preview of a film, showing some of its scenes

turkey film that few people went to see

tycoon successful and powerful business person

typecast when an actor is given very similar roles to play, over and over again

vintage clothes good-quality secondhand clothes

voice-over voice given to a cartoon character

volunteer person who works for free

zombie dead body brought back to life by supernatural powers

Index

Titles in the *Star Files* series include:

Hardback   1 844 43829 5

Hardback   1 844 43830 9

Hardback   1 844 43833 3

Hardback   1 844 43834 1

Hardback   1 844 43831 7

Hardback   1 844 43832 5

Find out about the other titles in this series on our website www.raintreepublishers.co.uk